To
_____

From
_____

A Little Spoonful of Chicken Soup for the Kid's Soul™

Published by Blessings Unlimited, Pentagon Towers
P.O. Box 398004, Edina, MN 55439

Design by Lecy Design

ISBN 1-58375-545-4
Printed in Mexico

A
Little
Spoonful
of
Chicken
Soup for the
Kid's Soul™

Thank you

For teaching me wrong
from right and encouraging
me to keep my dreams
in sight
  For showing me to not
let obstacles keep me down
  And for creating a smile
from my frown
  For saying that you care
about me

And for showing just how
special love should be
    For wiping my tears away
when I'm feeling sad
    And for calming me down
when I tend to get mad
    For helping others with
the good that you do
    And for teaching me that
I should help others, too

For hugging me when I
am feeling blue
   And whispering into my
ear "I love you"
   Thank you, family, for
all that you do
   I don't know where I
would be if it weren't
for you.

James Malinchak
Chicken Soup for the Kid's Soul

A Famous Father

A great man died today. He wasn't a world leader or a famous doctor or a war hero or a sports figure. He was no business tycoon, and you will never see his name in the financial pages. But he was one of the greatest men who ever lived. He was my father.

I guess you might say he was a person who was never

interested in getting credit or receiving honors. He did corny things like pay his bills on time, go to church on Sunday and serve as an officer in the P.T.A. He helped his kids with their homework and drove his wife to do the grocery shopping on Thursday nights. He got a great kick out of hauling his teenagers and their friends to and from football games.

Tonight is my first night without him. I don't know what to do with myself. I am sorry now for the times I didn't show him the proper respect. But I am grateful for a lot of other things.

I am thankful that God let me have my father for 15 years. And I am happy that I was able to let him know how much I loved him. That wonderful man died with a smile on his face and fulfillment in his heart. He knew that he was a great success as a husband and a father, a brother, a son and a friend. I wonder how many millionaires can say that?

Author Unknown

*I have learned to find
self-esteem in the things that make
me special and not in what others
say or don't say about me.*

Robert Diehl
Chicken Soup for the Kid's Soul

The Day I Figured Out That No One Is Perfect

Once there was a girl in my class that I thought was beautiful and smart. I believed that she was perfect. When it came time for my birthday, I invited her to my party, and she came.

A few months later, it was her birthday. I got a special necklace for her. Thinking about how happy she would be to receive my gift made me so excited.

I asked her when her birthday party was going to be. She replied, "Why do you want to know? You're not invited. You're just a dork with glasses!"

I felt really bad when she said that. I just stood there looking at her. Everyone standing by her came to stand next to me. Then we all left.

That day I figured out that even if someone looks perfect, there is a very good possibility that they aren't. When it comes to perfection, it's how someone treats you that is more important than how they look.

Ellie Logan (age 9)
Chicken Soup for the Kid's Soul

The
Sandbox

One day, when I was five, I went to a local park with my mom. While I was playing in the sandbox, I noticed a boy about my age in a wheelchair. I went over to him and asked if he could play. Since I was only five, I couldn't understand why he couldn't just get in the sandbox and play with me.

He told me he couldn't. I talked to him for a while longer, then I took my large bucket, scooped up as much sand as I could and dumped it into his lap. Then I grabbed some toys and put them in his lap, too.

My mom rushed over and said, "Lucas, why did you do that?"

I looked at her and replied, "He couldn't play in the sandbox with me, so I brought the sand to him. Now we can play in the sand together."

Lucas Parker (age 11)
Chicken Soup for the Kid's Soul

A French Accent

Last summer my family and I went to the beach for a camping trip. When we arrived at the camp-ground, all my cousins, aunts, uncles, and even my grandparents were there. After we got the tent set up, the adults started to make dinner. All of the kids went down to the river.

When we arrived, there were some older kids throwing rocks in the river, so we decided to go downriver a little. As we turned around to leave, my little ten-year-old cousin was already having a blast. He was yelling and throwing rocks in the river. My cousin has a speech problem, so he speaks in a kind of a funny way.

As we were walking away, the older kids started laughing at my cousin. They were teasing him and making fun of how he talks. At first he started to get really upset, but then he turned around and asked them why they were laughing. They told him that he talked stupidly. Then he asked them, "What, haven't you ever heard a French accent before?"

They just stood there for a minute with dumb looks on their faces and finally just walked away.

Erin Althauser (age 13)
Chicken Soup for the Kid's Soul

Everyone has something

to give.

Barbara Bush

I Found a Tiny starfish

I found a tiny starfish
In a tidepool by the sand.
I found a tiny starfish
And I put him in my hand.

An itty-bitty starfish
No bigger than my thumb,
A wet and golden starfish
Belonging to no one.

I thought that I
would take him
From the tidepool
by the sea,
And bring him home
to give to you
A loving gift from me.

But as I held my starfish,
His skin began to dry

Without his special
seaside home,
My gift to you would die.

I found a tiny starfish
in a tidepool by the sea.
I hope whoever finds
him next
Will leave him there,
like me!

And the gift I've saved
for you?
The best that I can give:
I found a tiny starfish,
And for you, I let him live.

Dayle Ann Dodds
Chicken Soup for the Kid's Soul

Do your best and
God will do the rest.

Debbie Herman
Chicken Soup for the Kid's Soul

A Good reason to Look up

When I was in junior high school, what my friends thought of me was real important to me. During those years I grew much taller than most of my peers. Being so tall made me feel uncomfortable. In order to keep the focus off of me and my unusual height, I went along with the crowd who would play practical jokes on other kids at school. Being one of the class clowns gave me a way to make sure that the jokes were directed at others, and not at me.

I would pull all kinds of pranks that were hurtful, and sometimes even harmful, to others....

My parents didn't always think that my behavior was funny. They reminded me about The Golden Rule: to treat others as I would like to be treated. Many times, I was disciplined for the hurtful ways that I was treating others. What I was doing was hurting other kids, and in turn hurting my reputation as someone to be looked up to. My friends were looking up to me because I was tall, but what did they see?

My parents wanted me to be a leader who was a good example to others—to be a decent human being. They taught me to set my own goals, and to do the best at everything that I set out to do. During the lectures I got from my father, he told me over and over again to be the leader that I was meant to be—to be a big man in my heart and actions, as well as in my body. I had to question myself whether or not it was important to be the kind of leader and person my father believed I was inside. I knew in my heart that he was right. So I tried my best to follow my father's advice.

Once I focused on being the best that I could be at basketball and became a leader in the game, I took my responsibility to set a good example more seriously. I sometimes have to stop and think before I act, and I make mistakes occasionally—everyone is human. But I continue to look for opportunities where I can make a difference, and to set a good example because of my father's advice. I now pass it on to you.

"Be a leader, Shaq, not a follower. Since people already have to look up to you, give them a good reason to do so."

Shaquille O'Neal
Chicken Soup for the Kid's Soul

*What's important in life
is how we treat each other.*

Hana Ivanhoe (age 15)

Father's Day

When I was six years old,
I never thought I would
feel happy inside again. My
father had just died. He had
been sick for a very long
time and never could play
with me....

Then the most wonderful
thing happened. My mom met
Michael. On New Year's Eve,
we all sat down together

and said our thanks for the past year and our wishes for the New Year. I told Michael that my wish was that he would be a dad to me. Michael's eyes filled with tears, and he said yes—but only if he could really be a father to me, not just do all the fun stuff. I said yes....

I want to thank Michael for being my dad, for being there for me and for taking away much of the sadness. I want to thank Michael for getting Mom to say yes to a lizard, for throwing a baseball with me and for being at all of my soccer games. But mostly I want to thank Michael for teaching me that parents can come to us in many different ways, and that a person who did not help to create you can be as much or more of a parent to you as someone who did. Happy Father's Day, Dad!

Taylor Martini, age 8
Chicken Soup for the Kid's Soul

The man who knows right from
wrong and has good
judgment and common sense
is happier than the man
who is immensely rich!
For such wisdom is far more
valuable than precious jewels.

Proverbs 3:13-15

Just a slight

Misunderstanding

In my class, when a person has a birthday, instead of being given a present, the birthday person brings a book to our class for the in-room library. On my birthday, I chose my favorite book: *There's a Boy in the Girls' Bathroom.*

I went to the bookstore and asked the lady behind

the counter, "Do you carry *There's a Boy in the Girls' Bathroom?* Instead of looking it up on the computer as I thought she would, she said, "Just a minute," and she disappeared. My mom and I waited and waited.

Finally she came back, and she said to me, "There's no one there now—he must have gone home with his mother."

I started laughing, and so did my mom. The lady was embarrassed—I guess she hadn't heard me say the words, "Do you carry?" She had been gone that entire time, looking for a boy in the girls' bathroom.

Melanie Hansen (age 10)
Chicken Soup for the Kid's Soul

Dear Momma

Dear Momma,

I miss you. I miss all the good things that we used to do. I miss how you would laugh and tuck me into bed. I miss your kisses and hugs. I miss the way you would talk about how you loved your kids and your family. You said if you were God, you wouldn't leave us.

Every night I think I see you and hear your voice, but I guess I really don't. Momma, I know you hear and see everything I say and do. Sometimes I want to cry, but I try to hold it in. Momma, I love you from the bottom of my heart. Your love is deep in my heart. I wish I could see you just one more time.

I wish you didn't have to die. I'll love you always. Your Son

Darnell Hill (age 13)
Chicken Soup for the Kid's Soul

Goooaaalllll!

Running as fast as my small legs could carry me, I concentrated on the black-and-white object spinning ahead, and realized that this was my chance.... I saw the faces of my opponents and could tell that some of them were running really hard. They wanted the ball, but it was mine, *all mine!*...

The other players gained on me, but I was nearing the goal. The confused look on the goalie's face told me that he wasn't ready to make a save. The rooting section on the sideline was chanting, "Kick it! Kick it! Kick the ball!"

I wound up and toed the ball as hard as a four-year-old ever could. It bounced into the net, past the scrambling goalie. I went wild! I had just scored my first real goal!

I ran back to my team-mates. Some were cheering and celebrating with me, but most of them had their arms crossed, with scowls on their faces and annoyed

looks in their eyes.
They wanted to score that goal, but I had! Ha! Ha!!
I looked to my mom and dad on the sideline. They were laughing with some other parents. This is just too cool! I'd scored my first ever goal—*for the other team!*

Heather Thomsen, age 13
Chicken Soup for the Kid's Soul

It's only in thy mind's eye that one can see rightly.

Antoine de Saint-Exupéry

A friend likes you for who you are
and not what you look like,
because that is what really matters.

Marleigh Dunlap (age 11)
Chicken Soup for the Kid's Soul